MACMILLAN
MUSIC and YOU

Piano Accompaniments

GRADE 2

Barbara Staton, Senior Author
Merrill Staton, Senior Author
Marilyn Davidson
Phyllis Kaplan

Susan Snyder, contributing author

Macmillan Publishing Company
New York

Collier Macmillan Publishers
London

Cover Design and Illustration: Heather Cooper
1991 Printing

Macmillan Publishing Company
866 Third Avenue
New York, N.Y. 10022
Collier Macmillan Canada, Inc.

Printed in the United States of America

ISBN: 0-02-294030-8
9 8 7 6 5

contents

The page number below the song title indicates the page in the pupil's edition where the song is found. For convenience, endings of melodic lines in the pupil's edition are indicated above the piano accompaniment by the symbol (▼). For example, (▼) indicates the end of the first line of music in the pupil's edition. The order of the piano accompaniments has been shifted where necessary to avoid page turns. The piano accompaniments do not always follow the chord structure of the pupil's edition.

Hello, There!

page 3

America

page 4

Music by Henry Carey
Words by Samuel F. Smith

1. My coun - try, 'tis of thee, Sweet land of
2. Our fa - ther's God, to Thee, Au - thor of

lib - er - ty, Of thee I sing. Land where my
lib - er - ty, To Thee we sing; Long may our

fa - thers died, Land of the Pil - grims' pride,
land be bright With Free - dom's ho - ly light;

From ev - 'ry moun - tain - side Let freedom ring.
Pro - tect us by Thy might, Great God, our King!

Old King Glory
page 6

Traditional
Piano accompaniment by William N. Simon

Old King Glo - ry of the moun -

tain. The moun - tain reached so high, it

near - ly reached the sky. The first one, the

sec - ond one, the third fol - low me.

If You're Happy

page 17

Clickety Clack

page 12

Music by Hap Palmer
Words by Martha and Hap Palmer
Piano accompaniment by Barbara Gastaldo

The Witch Rides

page 30

Music by Grace M. Meserve
Verses 1 and 3 by Grace M. Meserve
Verses 2 and 4 by Mary Jaye

1. The witch is on her broom - stick
2. See the ghosts come float - ing
3. The skel - e - ton is danc - ing
4. See the fun - ny gob - lins

Rid - ing ver - y fast, Oo - oo,
White a - gainst the sky, Oo - oo,
On his bon - y toes, Tip - ping,
Danc - ing down the street, Knock - ing,

Oo - oo Hal - low - een at last.
Oo - oo They go drift - ing by.
tap - ping, On and on he goes.
knock - ing, Cry - ing "Trick or treat."

False Face

page 40

Looby Loo

page 42

The Pumpkin in the Patch

page 45

Traditional Melody

4. The bat calls a ghost. . .

5. The ghost scares us all. . .

6. We all scare the ghost. . .

Barnyard Song

page 52

Kentucky Mountain Song

Bingo

page 57

Traditional Folk Melody

(You may wish to use this accompaniment with "Rondo" on page 170.)

Harvest

page 58

Danish Folk Song
Words Adapted

When all the leaves are turn-ing brown and ap - ple trees are bend-ing down, It's

time to pick the ap - ples sweet and gath - er in the har - vest.

Come and pick the ap - ples sweet, ap - ples sweet, ap - ples sweet.

Reach up high and don't be shy or you will be the last to eat.

She'll Be Comin' Round the Mountain

page 60

Southern Mountain Song

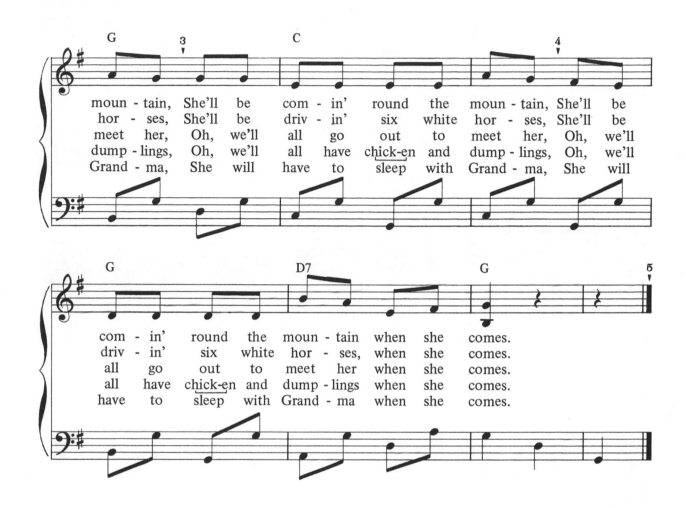

Over the River and Through the Wood

page 66

Traditional Melody
Words by Lydia Maria Childs
Piano accompaniment by Kryste Andrews

how the wind does blow!
grand-moth - er's face I spy!

It stings the toes and bites the nose As
Hur - rah for the fun! Is the pud - ding done? Hur -

o - ver the ground we go.
rah for the pump - kin pie!

Five Fat Turkeys

page 68

Traditional
Piano accompaniment by Kryste Andrews

Five fat tur-keys are we,____ We slept all night in a tree.____ When the cook came a-round we could-n't be found, So that's why we're here, you see.____

A la Puerta del Cielo

page 82

Spanish Folk Song

Jingle Bells

page 76

Words and music by
James Pierpont

Dash-ing through the snow, In a one-horse o-pen sleigh,

O'er the fields we go, Laugh-ing all the way;

Bells on bob-tail ring, Mak-ing spir-its bright, What

fun it is to ride and sing A sleigh-ing song to-night!

A Time for Love
page 79

Words and music by
Nancy Dervan

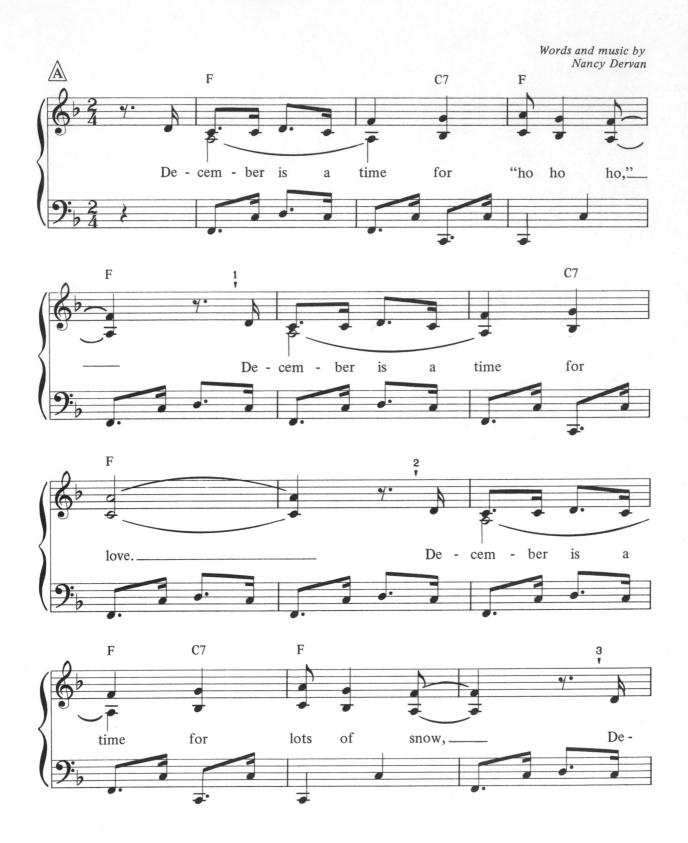

De - cem - ber is a time for "ho ho ho,"____

____ De - cem - ber is a time for

love._____ De - cem - ber is a

time for lots of snow,____ De -

Hanukah Song

page 80

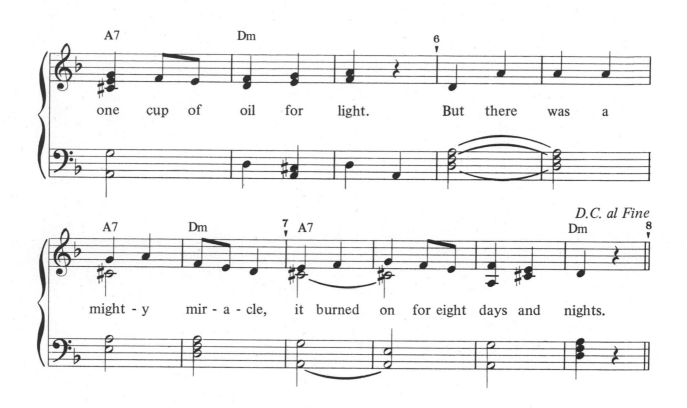

one cup of oil for light. But there was a

D.C. al Fine

might - y mir - a - cle, it burned on for eight days and nights.

Jolly Old Saint Nicholas

page 84

Traditional Carol
Piano accompaniment by William N. Simon

1. Jol - ly old Saint Nich - o - las, Lean your ear this way!
2. When the clock is strik - ing twelve, When I'm fast a - sleep,
3. John - ny wants a pair of skates, Su - sie wants a sled,

Don't you tell a sin - gle soul What I'm going to say;
Down the chim - ney broad and black, With your pack you'll creep.
Nel - lie wants a sto - ry - book, One she has - n't read.

Christ - mas Eve is com - ing soon; Now, you dear old man,
All the stock - ings you will find, Hang - ing in a row,
Now I think I'll leave to you What to give the rest,

Whis - per what you'll bring to me, Tell me, if you can.
Mine will be the short - est one, You'll be sure to know.
Choose for me, dear San - ta Claus, What you think is best.

Chicken Soup with Rice

page 108

Music by Carole King
Words by Maurice Sendak

What You Gonna Call Your Pretty Little Baby?

page 86

We Wish You a Merry Christmas
page 94

Traditional English Carol
Piano accompaniment by William N. Simon

Shake My Sillies Out

page 116

Music by Raffi
Words by Bert and Bonnie Simpson
Piano accompaniment by Lynn Freeman Olson

1. Got - ta shake, shake, shake my sil - lies out,
2. Got - ta clap, clap, clap my cra - zies out,

Shake, shake, shake my sil - lies out,
Clap, clap, clap my cra - zies out,

Shake, shake, shake my sil - lies out and
Clap, clap, clap my cra - zies out and

wig - gle my wag - gles a - way.
wig - gle my wag - gles a - way.

3.   Gotta jump, jump, jump my jiggles out. . .

4. *(slower)* Gotta yawn, yawn, yawn my sleepies out. . .

5.   Gotta shake, shake, shake my sillies out. . .

Jim Along, Josie

Page 110

American Folk Song
Piano accompaniment by William N. Simon

Face to the cen - ter, hands on your knees,

Clap three times and turn a - round, please!

D.C. al Fine

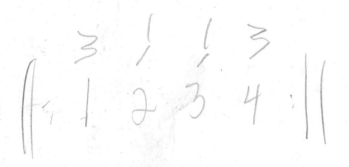

Martin Luther King

page 118

Words and music by
Theresa Fulbright

1. He want-ed peace and love all o-ver this
2. He walked for you and me all o-ver this
3. He died for free dom's cause to save ___ this

land, He want-ed peace and love all o-ver this
land, He walked for you and me all o-ver this
land, He died for free - dom's cause to save ___ this

The More We Get Together

page 120

German Folk Song

Grizzly Bear
page 129

Words and music by
Erling Bisgaard and Gulle Stehouwer
Piano accompaniment by William N. Simon

Griz - zly bear, a griz-zly bear is sleep-ing in a cave.

Please be ver - y qui - et, ver - y, ver - y qui - et,

If you wake him, if you shake him, he gets ver - y MAD!

It's So Nice on the Ice

page 124

Words and music by
Richard M. Sherman and Robert B. Sherman
Piano accompaniment by Barbara Gastaldo

Time to Wake Up!

page 130

I Made a Valentine

page 142

Words and music by
Lynn Freeman Olson

There's a Little Wheel A-Turnin' in My Heart

page 144

African American Folk Song

When You Send a Valentine

page 147

Words and music by
Mildred J. Hill and Louella Garrett

When you send a Val - en - tine, That's the time for fun. Push it un - der - neath the door, Ring the bell and run, run, run, run. Ring the bell and run.

Shoo, Fly

page 148

American Folk Song

Shoo, fly, don't both-er me, Shoo, fly, don't both-er me,

Shoo, fly, don't both-er me, For I be-long to some-bo-dy. I

feel, I feel, I feel, I feel like a morn-ing star, I

feel, I feel, I feel, I feel, I feel like a morn-ing star. Oh,

Shoo, fly, don't both - er me, Shoo, fly, don't both - er me,

Shoo, fly, don't both - er me, For I be-long to some-bo - dy.

We Love the U.S.A.

page 150

Music by John Philip Sousa
Words by Beatrice Krone
Piano accompaniment by Lynn Freeman Olson

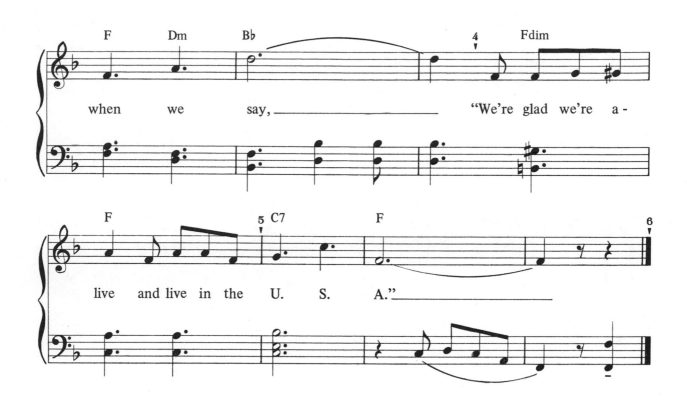

when we say, "We're glad we're a - live and live in the U. S. A."

Yankee Doodle

page 153

Old Woman and the Pig

page 158

Bluebird, Bluebird

page 159

Texas Folk Song

We Are Good Musicians
page 166

German Folk Song

Group: Oh, we are good mu-si-cians and we play in the band.
Group: We'll dem-on-strate our in-stru-ments so you will un-der-stand.

Solo: I play the trum-pet. Lis-ten to the trum-pet.
Group: We play the trum-pet. Lis-ten to the trum-pets. Ta-

Solo: ta-ta-ta, Ta-ta-ta-ta, Ta-ta-ta-ta-ta-ta. Ta-ta.
Group: ta-ta-ta, Ta-ta-ta-ta, Ta-ta-ta-ta-ta-

2. I play the drum.
   We play the drum. Listen to the...
   Boom-boom...

3. I play the piccolo.
   We play the piccolo. Listen to the...
   Toot-toot...

4. *Solo:* Ich bin ein Musikante, und komm aus Schwabenland.
   Group: Wir sind die Musikanten, und komm'n aus Schwabenland.
   Solo: Ich kann spielen, *Group:* Wir können spielen
   Solo: Auf der Trompete *Group:* Auf der Trompete.
   Solo: Ta-ra-ta-ta, Ta-ra-ta-ta, Ta-ra-ta-ta-ta-ta.
   Group: Ta-ra-ta-ta, Ta-ra-ta-ta, Ta-ra-ta-ta-ta.

Hear the Bells Ring

page 174

Words and music by
Konnie Saliba

John the Rabbit

page 172

American Folk Game Song
Piano accompaniment by William N. Simon

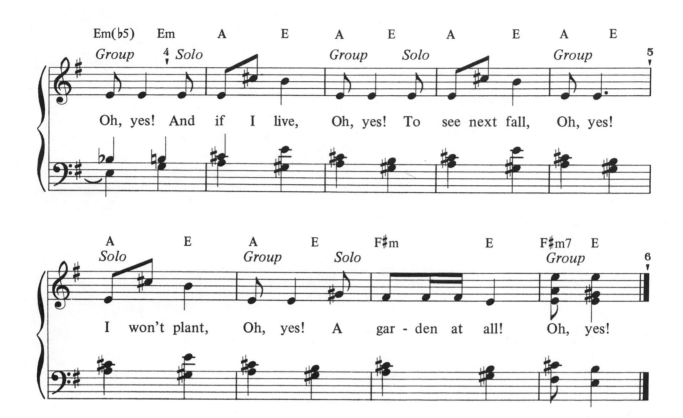

Mister Rabbit

page 176

African American Play Song
Piano accompaniment by Kryste Andrews

Verse

1. "Mis-ter Rab-bit, Mis-ter Rab-bit, your ears might-y long!"
2. "Mis-ter Rab-bit, Mis-ter Rab-bit, your foot's might-y red!"
3. "Mis-ter Rab-bit, Mis-ter Rab-bit, your coat's might-y gray!"
4. "Mis-ter Rab-bit, Mis-ter Rab-bit, your tail's might-y white!"

"Yes, in-deed, they're put on wrong."___
"Yes, in-deed, I'm al-most dead."___
"Yes, in-deed, 'twas made that way."___
"Yes, in-deed, I'm going out of sight."___

Refrain

Ev-'ry lit-tle soul must shine, shine, shine.___

Ev-'ry lit-tle soul must shine,___ shine, shine.

Michael Finnigin

page 187

American Folk Song
Piano accompaniment by Kryste Andrews

1. There was an old man named Mi - chael Fin - ni - gin.
2. There was an old man named Mi - chael Fin - ni - gin.
3. There was an old man named Mi - chael Fin - ni - gin.

He had whis - kers on his chin - i - gin.
Built a house of sticks and tin a - gain.
Went out fish - ing with a pin a - gain.

Wind blew them off but they grew in a - gain.
Wind came a - long and blew it in a - gain.
Caught a _____ whale that jumped back in a - gain.

Poor old Mi - chael Fin - ni - gin! Be - gin a - gain!
Poor old Mi - chael Fin - ni - gin! Be - gin a - gain!
Poor old Mi - chael Fin - ni - gin! Be - gin a - gain!

Y'a un Rat

page 180

French Traditional
Piano accompaniment by Kryste Andrews

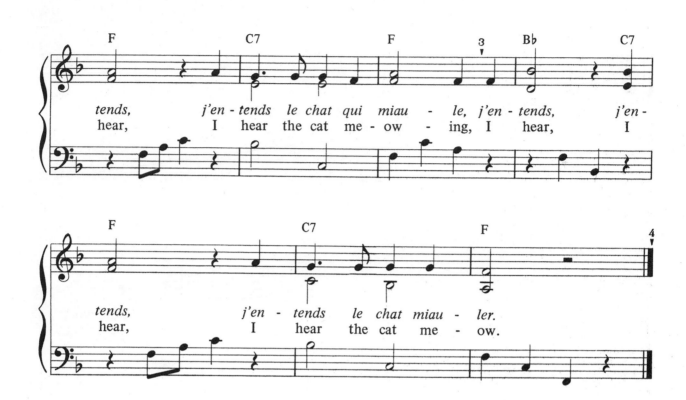

tends,   j'en - tends   le   chat   qui   miau - le,   j'en - tends,   j'en -
hear,   I   hear   the   cat   me - ow - ing,   I   hear,   I

tends,   j'en - tends   le   chat   miau - ler.
hear,   I   hear   the   cat   me - ow.

Let's Go Fly a Kite

page 184

Music by Richard M. Sherman
Words by Robert B. Sherman

1. With tup-pence for pa-per and strings, _____ You can
2. When you send _____ it fly-ing up there, _____ All at

have your own set of wings; _____ With your
once you're light-er than air; _____ You can

feet on the ground you're a bird in flight With your
dance on the breeze o-ver hous-es and trees With your

fist hold-ing tight _____ to the string of your kite.
fist hold-ing tight _____ to the string of your kite.

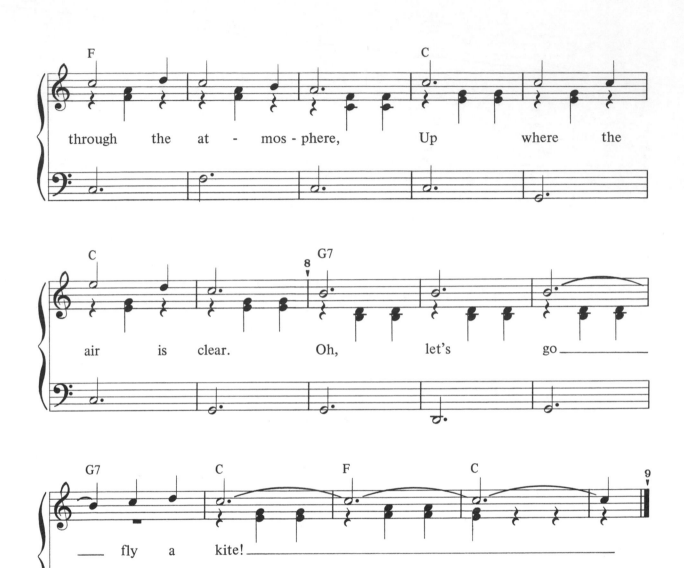

through the at - mos - phere, Up where the air is clear. Oh, let's go ____ fly a kite! ____

Who's That Tapping at the Window?

page 200

High Is Better Than Low
page 194

Words and music by
Howard Dietz and
Arthur Schwartz

rec - om-mend _ Sing wher-ev-er you go,

High is bet-ter than low, You'll be bet-ter if

you say it's so. _____

One Day My Mother Went to the Market

page 206

Italian Folk Song
Words by Leo Israel

Going over the Sea

page 211

Canadian Street Rhyme
Piano accompaniment by Lynn Freeman Olson

1. When I was one I ate a bun, Go - ing o - ver the
2. When I was two I buck-led my shoe, Go - ing o - ver the

sea.}
sea.}
I jumped a - board a sail - or - man's ship, And the

sail - or - man said to me, "Go - ing o - ver, go - ing

un - der, Stand at at - ten - tion like a

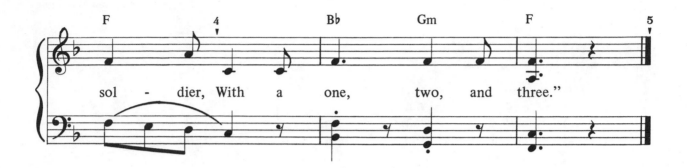

sol - dier, With a one, two, and three."

3. When I was three I banged my knee,
4. When I was four I shut the door,
5. When I was five I learned to jive,
6. When I was six I picked up sticks,

7. When I was seven I went to heaven,
8. When I was eight I learned to skate,
9. When I was nine I climbed a vine,
10. When I was ten I caught a hen,

Matarile

page 212

Mexican Folk Song

1. ¿Qué quiere usted? Ma-ta-ri-le, ri-le, ri-le.
   Quie-ro sal-tar, Ma-ta-ri-le, ri-le, ri-le.
2. What do you want? Ma-ta-ri-le, ri-le, ri-le.
   I want to jump, Ma-ta-ri-le, ri-le, ri-le.

¿Qué quiere usted? Ma-ta-ri-le, ri-le, ron.
Quie-ro sal-tar, Ma-ta-ri-le, ri-le, ron.
What do you want? Ma-ta-ri-le, ri-le, ron.
I want to jump, Ma-ta-ri-le, ri-le, ron.

(Other verses) Quiero marchar. . .
Quiero correr. . .

Pop Goes the Weasel

page 213

American Singing Game

A pen - ny for a spool ___ of thread, A
pen - ny for a nee - dle. That's the way the
mon - ey goes, Pop! goes the wea - sel.

I May Be Old

page 218

Words and music by
John Horman

Lightly

Animals *mf*

1. *(Donkey)* I may be old, or so I'm told, But I can still do
   (I) may be old, or so I'm told, But I can still do
   (I) may be old, or so I'm told, But I can still do
   (I) may be old, or so I'm told, But I can still do
   (We) may be old, or so we're told, But we can still do

ma - ny things.__ My back's not strong, the road's too long,
ma - ny things.__ My bark is weak, my tail keeps beat,
ma - ny things.__ I won't catch mice, they seem so nice,
ma - ny things.__ I crow too loud! Be - cause I'm proud,
ma - ny things.__ Good friends are we, as you can see,

[Introduction, interludes, and ending not in the pupil's book.]

Three Men Sittin' at a Table

page 220

Giants! Giants!

page 224

Sing for Our Supper/Hee Haw

page 221

Words and music by
John Horman

Sing!   Sing our sweet song.

Dog

Hee   haw! Bow wow wow wow!

[Introduction and ending not in the pupil's book.]

Sit Down, Let's Eat

page 222

ser - e - nade is now com-plete!   The

food is here,   sit down, let's   eat!

A Robber Must Be Brave

page 223

Home, Sweet Home

page 225

We no far-ther now will roam. Four good friends,— home sweet home..

[Introduction and coda not in pupil's book.]

Good News

page 229

African American Spiritual

Good news! (clap clap) Char-i-ot's com-in', Good

news! (clap clap) Char-i-ot's com-in', Good news! (clap clap)

Char-i-ot's com-in' and I don't want it to leave me be-hind.

Rover
page 230

page 230

Traditional English Rhyme

1. I have a dog and his name is Ro - ver.
2. When he is good he is good all o - ver.

He is the one I love the best.
When he is bad he is just a pest.

Button, You Must Wander
page 231

page 231

Traditional
Piano accompaniment by
Kryste Andrews

But-ton, you must wan - der, wan - der, wan - der,

But - ton, you must wan - der ev - 'ry - where.

Rocky Mountain

page 230

Southern Folk Song

Battle Hymn of the Republic

page 232

Music by William Steffe
Words by Julia Ward Howe

America, the Beautiful

page 233

Music by Samuel Ward
Words by Katherine Lee Bates

1. O beau-ti-ful for spa-cious skies, For am-ber waves of grain, For pur-ple moun-tain maj-es-ties A-bove the fruit-ed plain! A-mer-i-ca! A-mer-i-ca! God shed His grace on thee And crown thy good with broth-er-hood From sea to shin-ing sea.

2. O beau-ti-ful for pa-triot dream That sees be-yond the years Thine al-a-bas-ter cit-ies gleam, Un-dimmed by hu-man tears!

There Are Many Flags in Many Lands

page 234

Composer Unknown
Words by M.H. Howliston

There are man-y flags in man-y lands, There are flags of ev-'ry hue; But there is no flag, how-ev-er grand, Like our own Red, White_ and_ Blue. Then hur-rah for the flag, Our coun-try's flag, Its stripes and white stars, too; For there is no flag in an-y land, Like our own Red, White_and_ Blue.

One Dark Night

page 236

Mary Had a Baby

page 241

Spiritual

5. Born in lowly stable...
6. Where did Mary lay him...
7. Laid him in a manger...

Must Be Santa

page 236

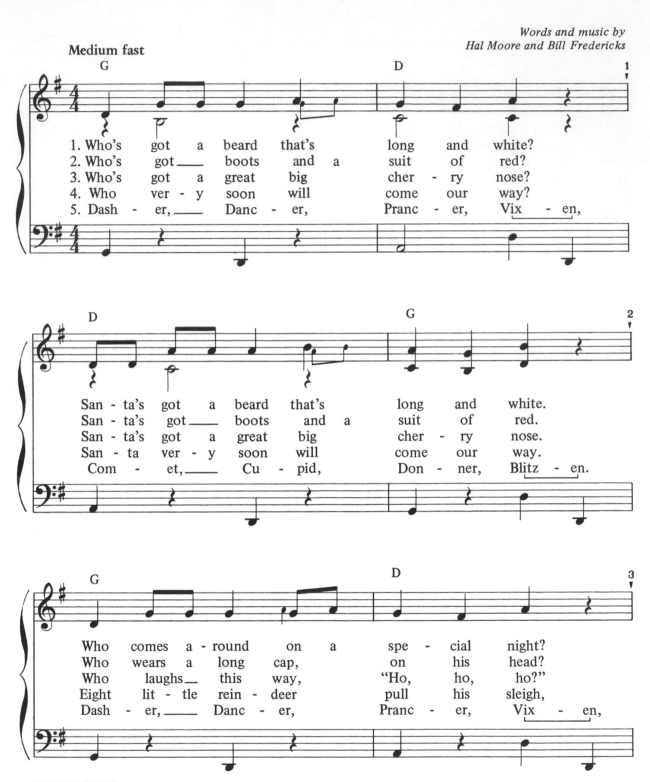

Up on the Housetop

page 239

Words and music by
Benjamin T. Hanby
Piano accompaniment by
Kryste Andrews

1. Up on the house-top the rein-deer pause,
2. First comes the stock-ing of lit-tle Nell;
3. Look in the stock-ing of lit-tle Bill;

Out jumps good old San-ta Claus; Down through the chim-ney with
Oh, dear San-ta, fill it well. Give her a dol-ly that
Oh, just see what a glo-ri-ous fill! Here is a ham-mer, and

lots of toys, All for the lit-tle ones' Christ-mas joys.
laughs and cries, One that can o-pen and shut its eyes.
lots of tacks, Whis-tle and a ball and a whip that cracks.

Hanukah

page 242

Hebrew Folk Song

Ha - nu - kah, Ha - nu - kah, mer - ry hol - i - day!

Ha - nu - kah, Ha - nu - kah, Time to dance and play.

Ha - nu - kah, Ha - nu - kah, bright the can - dles burn,

Round and round, round and round, Watch the drey - dl turn!

Little Candle Fires

page 243

Music by S.E. Goldfarb
Words by S.S. Grossman
Piano accompaniment by
Kryste Andrews

More verses may be added by using the numbers *three* through *eight.*

Do Your Ears Hang Low?

page 244

Traditional

The Bus

page 246

Play Song

I've a Pair of Fishes

page 247

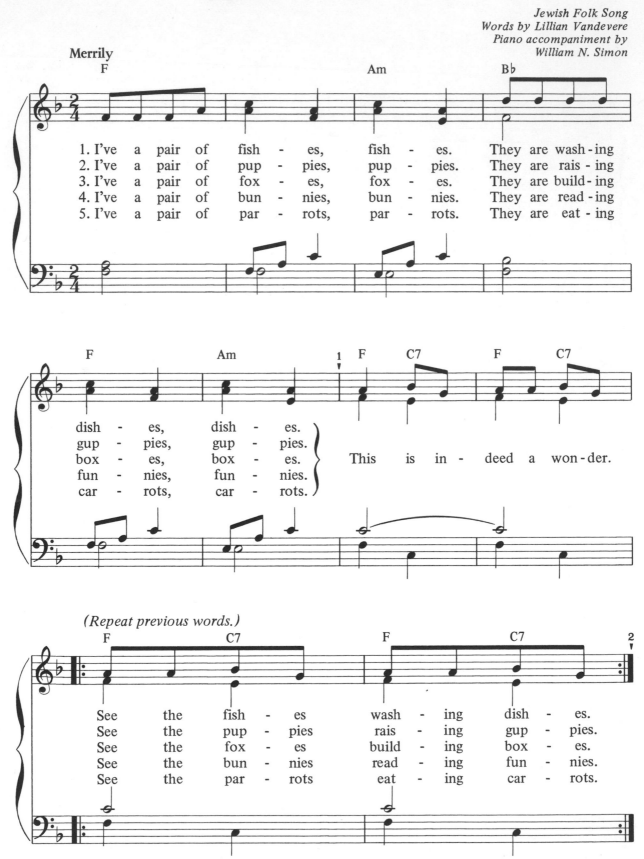

Lucy

page 248

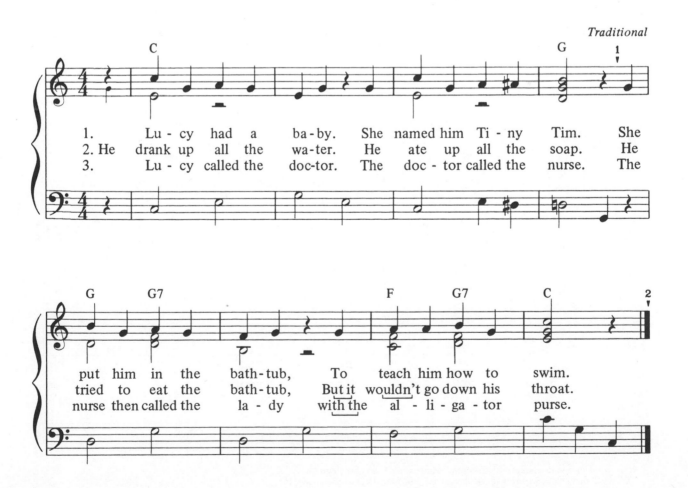

Dumplin's
page 248

Calypso Song from the West Indies

Ten in a Bed

page 252

Traditional
Piano accompaniment by
Kryste Andrews

1. There were ten in a bed and the lit - tle one said, "Roll o - ver! Roll
2. There were nine in a bed and the lit - tle one said, "Roll o - ver! Roll

o - ver!" So they all rolled o - ver and one fell out!
o - ver!" So they all rolled o - ver and one fell out!

Verses 3-9: There were (eight, seven, six, and so on)

10. There was one in a bed, and the lit - tle one said, "Good night!"

(spoken)

The Little Shoemaker

page 249

Traditional
Piano accompaniment by
Kryste Andrews

There's a lit-tle wee man in a lit-tle wee house, Lives o-ver the way you see, And he sits at the win-dow and sews all day, Mak-ing shoes for you and me. A-rap a-tap tap, A-rap a-tap tap, Hear the ham-mer's tit-tat-tee. A-rap a-tap tap, A-

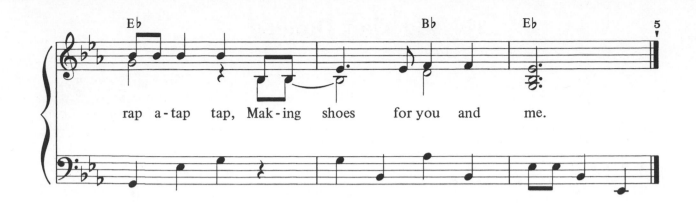

rap a-tap tap, Mak-ing shoes for you and me.

This Old Man
page 250

English Folk Song
Piano accompaniment by
Kryste Andrews

1. This old man, he played one, He played nick-nack on my drum.
2. This old man, he played two, He played nick-nack on my shoe.
3. This old man, he played three, He played nick-nack on my tree.
4. This old man, he played four, He played nick-nack on my door.

} With a

nick-nack pad-dy whack, give a dog a bone, This old man came roll-ing home.

5. This old man, he played five, He played nick-nack on my hive...
6. This old man, he played six, He played nick-nack on my sticks...
7. This old man, he played seven, He played nick-nack on my oven...
8. This old man, he played eight, He played nick-nack on my gate...
9. This old man, he played nine, He played nick-nack on my line...
10. This old man, he played ten, He played nick-nack on my hen...

And They Danced
page 253

Words and music by
Clara E. Spelman
Piano accompaniment by
Barbara Gastaldo

A fid-dler picked up his bow one day, And he fid-dled a-way. He fid-dled a-way, And he fid-dled and he fid-dled a-way. A

1. duck heard him play so the duck be-gan to say,
2. mouse heard him play so the mouse be-gan to say,
3. frog heard him play so the frog be-gan to say,
4. crick-et heard him play so the crick-et be-gan to say,
5. bee heard him play so the bee be-gan to say,

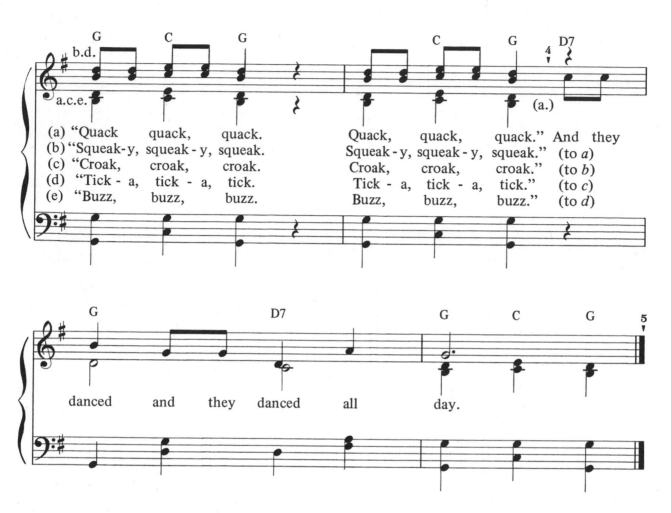

(a) "Quack   quack,   quack.   Quack,   quack,   quack." And they
(b) "Squeak-y, squeak-y, squeak.   Squeak-y, squeak-y, squeak." (to *a*)
(c) "Croak,   croak,   croak.   Croak,   croak,   croak." (to *b*)
(d) "Tick-a,   tick-a,   tick.   Tick-a,   tick-a,   tick." (to *c*)
(e) "Buzz,   buzz,   buzz.   Buzz,   buzz,   buzz." (to *d*)

danced   and   they   danced   all   day.

(Sing *quack* low, *squeaky* high, *croak* low, *ticka* high, and *buzz* low.)

Little Spotted Puppy

page 254

wig - gled his   ears,   and he   wag - gled his   tail,   And he
wig - gles his   ears,   and he   wag - gles his   tail,   And he

barked,   and he   barked!   'Cause he   wig-gled his   ears, and he
barks,   and he   barks!   So, he   wig-gles his   ears, and he

L.H. over

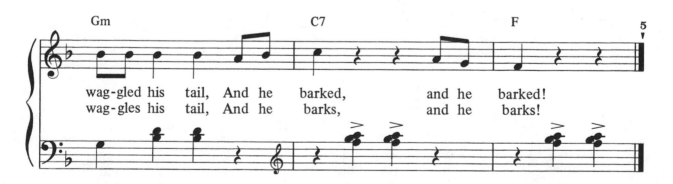

wag-gled his   tail, And he   barked,   and he   barked!
wag-gles his   tail, And he   barks,   and he   barks!

Little White Duck
page 255

Music by Bernard Zaritsky
Words by Walt Barrows

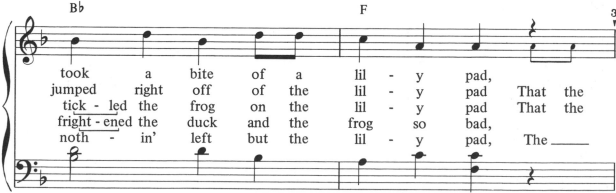

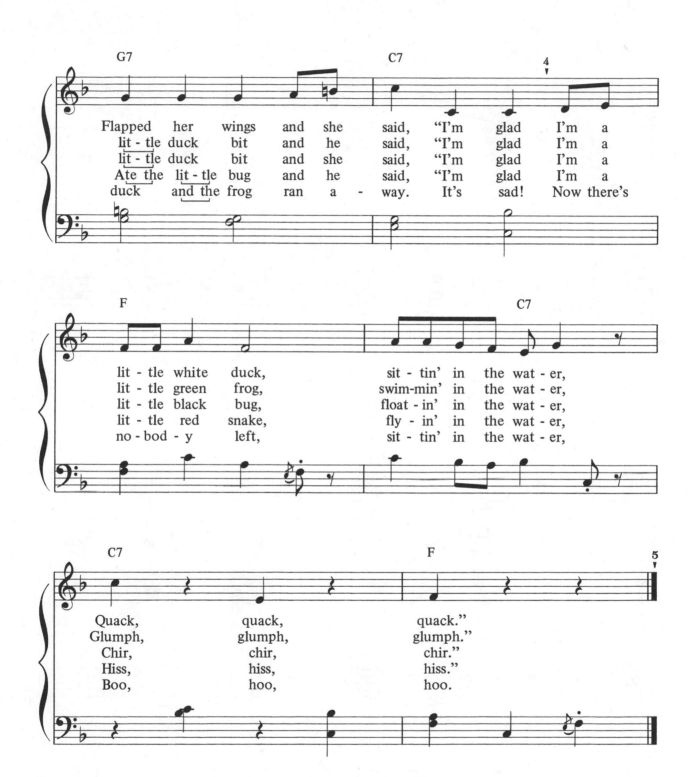

Flapped her wings and she said, "I'm glad I'm a
lit - tle duck bit and he said, "I'm glad I'm a
lit - tle duck bit and she said, "I'm glad I'm a
Ate the lit - tle bug and he said, "I'm glad I'm a
duck and the frog ran a - way. It's sad! Now there's

lit - tle white duck, sit - tin' in the wat - er,
lit - tle green frog, swim-min' in the wat - er,
lit - tle black bug, float - in' in the wat - er,
lit - tle red snake, fly - in' in the wat - er,
no - bod - y left, sit - tin' in the wat - er,

Quack, quack, quack."
Glumph, glumph, glumph."
Chir, chir, chir."
Hiss, hiss, hiss."
Boo, hoo, hoo.

Little Sir Echo

page 256

Words and music by Laura R. Smith and J.S. Fearis
Revised Arrangement by Adele Girard and Joe Marsala
Piano accompaniment by William N. Simon

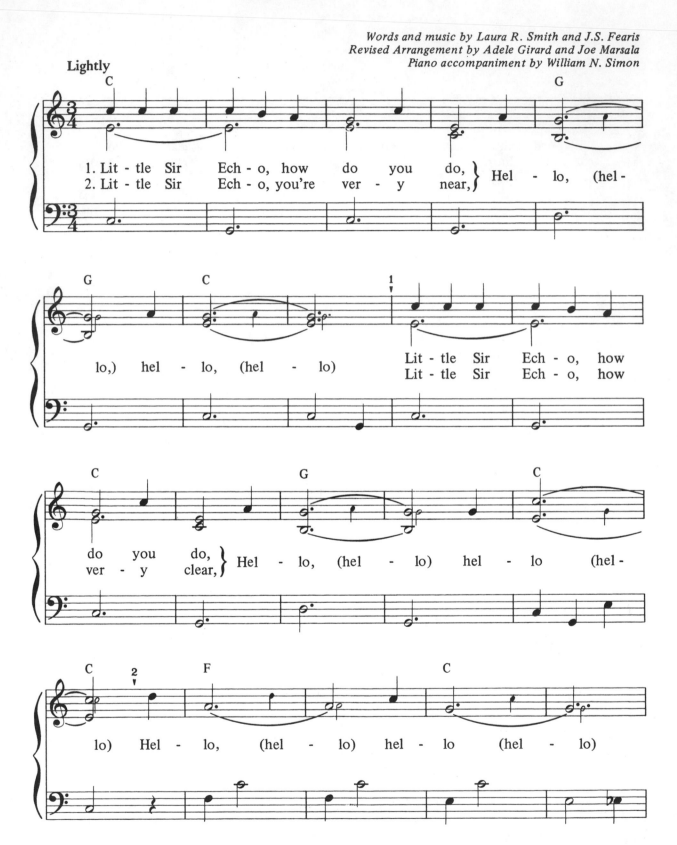

Won't you come o - ver and play?_____ You're a nice lit - tle

fel - low, I know by your voice, But you're al - ways so far a -

way. (a - way)   [Ending not in pupils' book.
                  May also be used as an introduction.]

Obwisana

page 257

La Muñeca

page 258

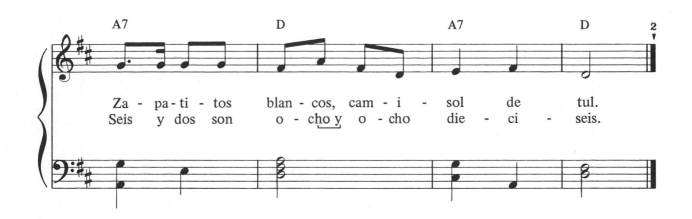

Za - pa - ti - tos blan - cos, cam - i - sol de tul.
Seis y dos son o - cho y o - cho die - ci - seis.

Michael, Row the Boat Ashore
page 258

Folk Song from the Bahamas

Mi - chael row the boat a - shore, Hal - le - lu - jah!

Mi - chael row the boat a - shore, Hal - le - lu - jah!

Supercalifragilisticexpialidocious
page 260

Music by Richard M. Sherman
Words by Robert B. Sherman

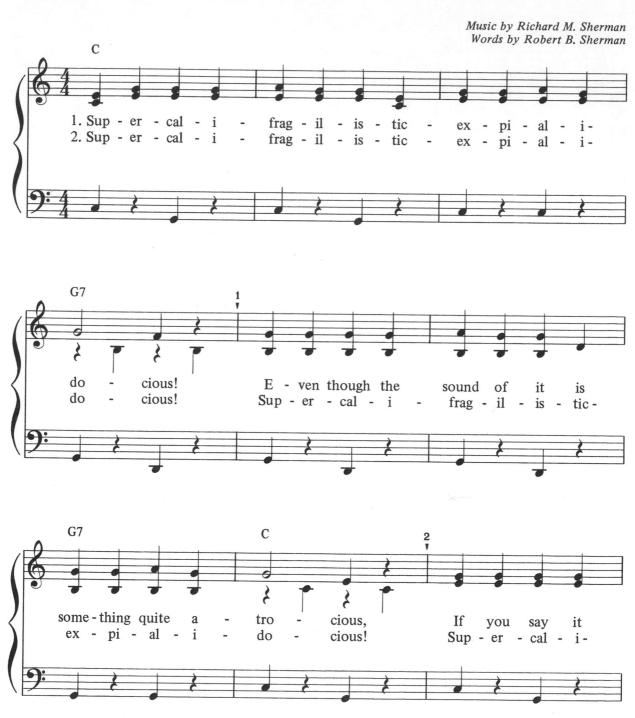

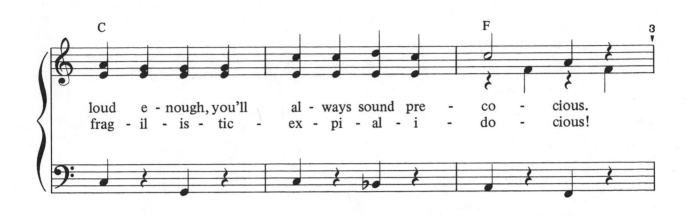

loud e - nough, you'll al - ways sound pre - co - cious.
frag - il - is - tic - ex - pi - al - i - do - cious!

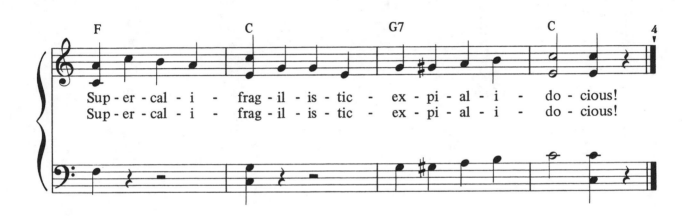

Sup - er - cal - i - frag - il - is - tic - ex - pi - al - i - do - cious!
Sup - er - cal - i - frag - il - is - tic - ex - pi - al - i - do - cious!

Shake the Papaya Down

page 259

Calypso Song
Collected by W.S. Haynie
Piano accompaniment by
Barbara Gastaldo

When the Train Comes Along

page 261

American Folk Song
Piano accompaniment by
Kryste Andrews

The Railroad Train

page 262

Words and music by
Charles Harvey
Piano accompaniment by
Barbara Gastaldo

1. Click - et - y clack, a - lunk, a - lunk! A
2. O - ver the bridge, a - cross the lake, A

train is com - ing, a - chunk, a - chunk; A click - et - y clack a
mile a min - ute, it has to make; A ter - ri - ble snake, with

mile a - way; It has - n't a sec - ond o'
flam - ing eyes, That wig - gles and wig - gles a -

All Night, All Day

page 264

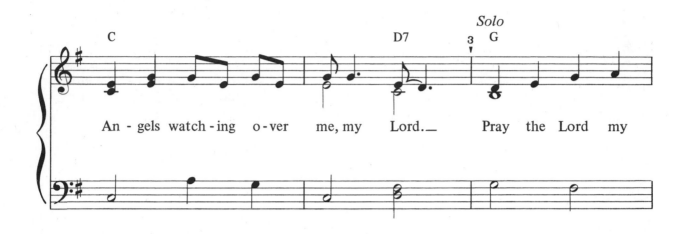

An - gels watch - ing o - ver me, my Lord.__ Pray the Lord my

soul __ to keep, An - gels watch - ing o - ver me.

Tender Shepherd

page 263

Music by Mark Charlap
Words by Carolyn Leigh

1. Ten - der shep - herd, ten - der shep - herd
2. Ten - der shep - herd, ten - der shep - herd

watch - es o - ver all his sheep. One, say your prayers and
you for - got to count your sheep. One, in the mea - dow;

two, close your eyes and three, safe and hap - pi - ly fall a - sleep.
two, in the gar - den; three, in the nur - ser - y fast a - sleep.

By'm Bye

page 265

Folk Song from Texas
Piano accompaniment by
Kryste Andrews

Bibbidi-Bobbidi-Boo

page 266

*Words and music by
Mack David, Al Hoffman,
and Jerry Livingston*

PA 130

Chicken Soup with Rice

page 268

Music by Carole King
Words by Maurice Sendak

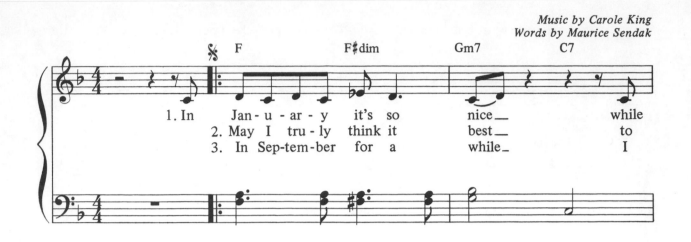

1. In Jan-u-ar-y it's so nice ___ while
2. May I tru-ly think it best ___ to
3. In Sep-tem-ber for a while ___ I

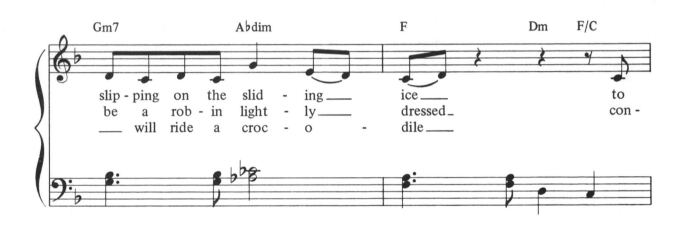

slip-ping on the slid-ing ___ ice ___ to
be a rob-in light-ly ___ dressed ___ con-
___ will ride a croc-o-dile ___

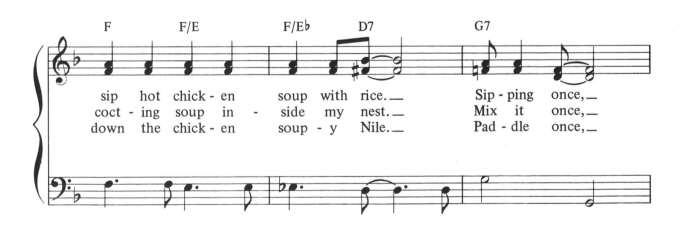

sip hot chick-en soup with rice. ___ Sip-ping once, ___
coct-ing soup in-side my nest. ___ Mix it once, ___
down the chick-en soup-y Nile. ___ Pad-dle once, ___

I Live in a City

page 270

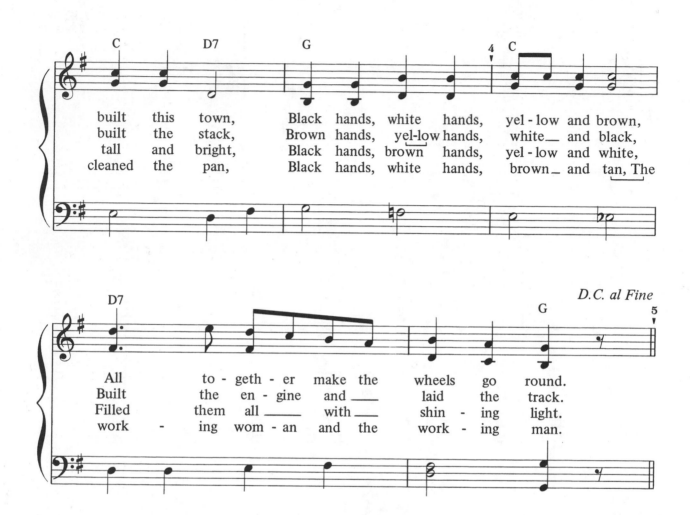

built   this   town,   Black   hands,   white   hands,   yel-low and brown,
built   the   stack,   Brown hands, yel-low hands, white and black,
tall   and   bright,   Black   hands, brown hands, yel-low and white,
cleaned the   pan,   Black   hands,   white   hands, brown and tan, The

D.C. al Fine

All   to-geth-er make the   wheels   go   round.
Built   the en-gine and   laid   the   track.
Filled   them all   with   shin-ing light.
work-ing wom-an and the   work-ing man.

Sing Me a Song

page 271

Words and music by
Barbara Staton

ACKNOWLEDGMENTS

Grateful acknowledgment is given to the following authors and publishers. In the case of songs for which acknowledgment is not given, we have earnestly endeavored to find the original source and to procure permission for their use, but without success. Extensive research failed to locate the author and/or copyright holder.

Alfred Publishing Company for *Clickety Clack* by Martha and Hap Palmer from HAP PALMER FAVORITES, 1981. Reprinted courtesy of the publisher.

Belwin Mills for *Little Spotted Puppy* and *I Made a Valentine* from SONGS FOR OUR SMALL WORLD by Lynn Freeman Olson and Georgia Garlid. Copyright © 1968 by Schmitt Music Center, a division of Belwin-Mills Publishing Corp. Used by permission. All rights reserved. For *Hear the Bells Ring* from SAFARI by Konnie Saliba. Copyright © 1976 by Belwin-Mills Publishing Corp. Used by permission. All rights reserved.

Birch Tree Group for *A La Puerta del Cielo*, music by Gladys Pitcher. Copyright © 1962 by Birch Tree Group Ltd. Used by permission. All rights reserved. For *I've a Pair of Fishes*, words by J. Lilian Vandevere. From Birchard Music Series Book 2. Copyright © 1962 by Birch Tree Group Ltd. Used by permission. All rights reserved.

Board of Jewish Education for *Little Candle Fires* from SONGS FOR CHILDREN by Hyman Reznick, composers S.E. Goldfarb and S.S. Grossman. Reprinted courtesy of the Board of Jewish Education.

Milton Bradley Co. for the words to *When You Send a Valentine* by Mildred J. Hill from Emilie Poulsson's HOLIDAY SONGS.

Nancy Dervan for *A Time for Love* from PIECES AND PROCESS NO. 4 "CHRISTMAS TIDINGS," 1980. Copyright © 1985 by Nancy Dervan. Reprinted by permission.

Theresa Fulbright for *Martin Luther King* from THE SPECTRUM OF MUSIC, Grade 2, by Marsh, Rinehart, and Savage, Copyright © 1974 Macmillan Publishing Co., Inc. Reprinted by permission.

Ginn & Co. for the music to *When You Send a Valentine* by Louella Garrett from "SINGING ON OUR WAY" of OUR SINGING WORLD series. Copyright © 1959, 1957, 1949, by Ginn & Co. Used by permission.

Harper & Row for *Our Flag* (first line "There Are Many Flags in Many Lands") by Mary Howliston from THE GOLDEN FLUTE, selected by Alice Hubbard and Adeline Babbitt (John Day Co.). Copyright © 1932, 1960 by Harper & Row, Publishers, Inc. Reprinted by permission of Harper & Row, Publishers, Inc.

W.S. Haynie for *Shake the Papaya Down* collected by W.S. Haynie. Copyright © 1966, Gulf Music Co. Used by permission.

D.C. Health & Company for *False Face* by David Russell and Susan Rupert from MUSIC FOR YOUNG AMERICANS by Richard Berg, Claudene Burns, Daniel Hooley, Robert Pace and Josephine Wolverton. By permission of D.C. Heath.

John Horman for *The Bremen Town Musicians*, Copyright © 1985 by John Horman.

Loghaven Music for *One Dark Night* by Lynn Freeman Olson. Copyright © 1986 by Loghaven Music (ASCAP).

MMB Music, Inc. for *Grizzly Bear* by Erling Bisgaard and Gulle Stehouwer from MUSICBOOK O. Copyright © 1976 by Magnamusic-Baton, Inc./Edition Wilhelm Hansen. Used by permission. Unauthorized reproduction prohibited.

Rockhaven Music for *Sing Me a Song* and *Time to Wake Up!* © 1987.

Schroder Music Co. for *I Live in a City*. Words and music by Malvina Reynolds. Copyright © 1960 by Schroder Music Co. Used by permission. All rights reserved.

Shawnee Press for *One Day My Mother Went to the Market* from LITTLE FOLK SONGS, collected and adapted by Rudolph Goehr. Copyright © 1958, 1961 by Shawnee Press, Inc., Deleware Water Gap, PA. International Copyright Secured. All rights reserved. Used by permission.

Silver, Burdett & Ginn Inc. for *The Bus* from *Singing On Our Way* of OUR SINGING WORLD SERIES. Copyright © 1949, 1957, 1959, by Silver, Burdett & Ginn Inc. Used by permission.

Warner Brothers for *Chicken Soup with Rice*. Lyric by Maurice Sendak, music by Carole King. Copyright © 1975 by COLGEMS-EMI MUSIC, INC., and ELORAC MUSIC. All administration rights controlled by COLGEMS-EMI MUSIC, INC. 6920 Sunset Blvd., Hollywood, CA 90028. All rights reserved. Used by permission. For *Little White Duck*, words by Walt Barrows, music by Bernard Zaritsky. Copyright © 1950 by COLGEMS-EMI MUSIC, INC. Copyright renewed 1977 by COLGEMS-EMI MUSIC, INC., Hollywood, CA. All rights reserved. Used by permission. For *High Is Better Than Low (From Jennie)* by Arthur Schwartz and Howard Dietz. Copyright © 1963 WARNER BROTHERS, INC. All rights reserved. Used by permission. For *Little Sir Echo*, original version by Laura Smith and J.S. Fearis. Verse and Revised Arrangement by Adele Girard and Joe Marsala. Copyright © 1917 FEARIS & BRO. Copyright renewed and assigned to WB MUSIC CORP. All rights reserved. Used by permission.

ALPHABETICAL SONG INDEX